MIGRATION

NATURE'S CYCLES

Mel Higginson

Rourke
Publishing LLC
Vero Beach, Florida 32964

www.rourkepublishing.com

PHOTO CREDITS: All Photographs © Lynn M. Stone, except P. 7 Mastana, P. 11 Philipdyer, P. 19 Daniel Brunner

Editor: Robert Stengard-Olliges

Cover and interior design by Nicola Stratford

Library of Congress Cataloging-in-Publication Data

Higginson, Mel.
  Migration / Mel Higginson.
     p. cm. -- (Nature's cycle)
  ISBN 1-60044-179-3 (hardcover)
  ISBN 1-59515-536-8 (softcover)
  1. Animal migration--Juvenile literature. I. Title. II. Series: Higginson, Mel. Nature's cycle.
  QL754.S76 2007
  591.56'8--dc22   2006014318

Printed in the USA

CG/CG

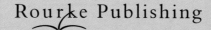

Rourke Publishing

www.rourkepublishing.com – sales@rourkepublishing.com
Post Office Box 3328, Vero Beach, FL 32964

Table of Contents

Why Animals Migrate

Migration is a long journey by animals. Migrations happen at about the same time each year.

Animals **migrate** to find better living. Better living often means finding plentiful food. But food is not the only reason animals migrate.

Some migrations are for the sake of baby animals. Adult humpback whales leave plentiful food in cold ocean water. They migrate to warm water.

Whales do not find as much food in warm water. But their calves would not survive if they were born in cold water.

Migrations: Round Trips

Animals that migrate usually stay in their new homes for several weeks or months. Then they return to where the migration began.

For example, many kinds of birds migrate south each autumn. They return north in spring.

Animals That Migrate

Other kinds of animals migrate, too. In addition to whales, some seals and fish migrate in the oceans.

Mountain sheep migrate down mountains, away from winter snow. Wildebeests in Africa migrate across rivers and grasslands. Wildebeests follow **seasonal** rains.

Monarch butterflies are among the few insects that migrate. Monarchs fly south each fall from the United States to Mexico.

Pacific salmon migrate from rivers to oceans. Years later they migrate back to rivers where they were born. There they lay eggs and die.

How Animals Migrate

Animals make long distance migrations using many **cues**. Some use the sun, moon, and stars as guides. Some follow rivers or mountains.

Salmon return to the smell of their home streams! Ocean movements may guide sea animals. Some animals seem to have a **magnetic compass**.

Migrations are more than nature's calendar.
Migrations help animals **survive**!

Glossary

cues (K YOOS) — a signal to do something

magnetic compass (MAG neh tik KUHM puhss) — an instrument for finding directions

migrate (MYE grate) — to move from one place to another

seasonal (SEE zuhn uhl) — related to the four seasons of the year

survive (sur VIVE) — to continue to live or exist

INDEX

FURTHER READING

Hoff, Mary. *Migration*. The Creative Company, 2002.
Rylant, Cynthia. *The Journey: Stories of Migration*. Scholastic, 2006.

WEBSITES TO VISIT

http://www.sciencemadesimple.com/animals.html

ABOUT THE AUTHOR

Mel Higginson writes children's nonfiction and poetry. This is Mel's first year writing for Rourke Publishing. Mel lives with his family just outside of Tucson, Arizona.